Take Your (Equally Horible) Pick!

TAKE YOUR PICK OF

MONSTER ENCOUNTERS

BY G.G. LAKE

CAPSTONE PRESS

a capstone imprint

Blazers Books are published by Capstone Press,
1710 Roe Crest Drive, North Mankato, Minnesota 56003
www.mycapstone.com

Library of Congress Cataloging-in-Publication Data
Cataloging-in-publication data is available on the Library of Congress website.
ISBN 978-1-5157-4472-6 (library binding)
ISBN 978-1-5157-4476-4 (paperback)
ISBN 978-1-5157-4488-7 (eBook PDF)

Get spooked as you compare and stare at some of the scariest monsters on the planet. From dragons and krakens to vampires and werewolves, which would you want to face?

Editorial Credits
Nikki Potts, editor; Kyle Grenz, designer; Tracey Engel, media researcher;
Kathy McColley, production specialist

Photo Credits
Alamy: Photo Researchers, Inc., 21; Shutterstock: Alexilusmedical, 25 (spine), Alexlky, 18, Barashkova Natalia, 11, 19, bluecrayola, 24, cristographic, 27, Dieter Hawlan, 14, Fotokostic, 8, gritsalak karalak, 5, Kiselev Andrey Valerevich, front cover (top), 12, Lightspring, back cover and spine, Linda Bucklin, 20, Lukiyanova Natalia/frenta, front cover (bottom), Margaret M Stewart, 6, Melkor3D, 15, Mike H, 26, Taras Stelmah, 17, Unholy Vault Designs, 25, Val Thoermer, 16 (background), Valery Sidelnykov, 16, Vuk Kostic, 7, 9; The Image Works: Fine Art Images/Heritage, 22, Musée Carnavalet/Roger-Viollet, 23, Painted by Anthony Wallis Fortean/TopFoto, 10; Wikimedia: Pieter Dirkx/CC-BY-SA-1.0, 13

Printed and bound in China.
007887

TABLE OF CONTENTS

MONSTER WALK

You walk along the road at night. Suddenly, you shiver. The hairs on the back of your neck rise. You know someone or something is watching you. It could be a number of monsters—all equally horrible. If you had to choose, which would you pick?

Many of the monsters in this book appear only in *myths* or stories. Others are *cryptids* that may or may not be real. But whether they are fact or fiction, they are all horrible!

myth—a story from ancient times

cryptid—a creature whose existence has not been proven by science

VAMPIRE VS. WEREWOLF

Would you rather face a vampire or a werewolf?

VAMPIRE

FOUND: TRANSYLVANIA, ROMANIA

▶ The speed and strength of vampires make them nearly impossible to kill.

▶ Vampires can change their shape. Wolves, bats, or clouds of mist could all be changed vampires.

▶ They use their **fangs** to drink blood and suck their victims dry.

fang—a long, pointed tooth

WEREWOLF
FOUND: WESTERN EUROPE

▶ A human becomes a werewolf either by a werewolf bite or from a witch's **curse**.

▶ Werewolves are excellent hunters. They have great strength and speed.

▶ Their hunger controls them. Werewolves are always looking for their next meal.

curse—an evil spell meant to harm someone

MINOTAUR vs. HARPY

Would you pick the Minotaur or a harpy?

MINOTAUR

FOUND: CRETE, GREECE

- ▶ The Minotaur is strong. It has the body of a man and the head and tail of a bull.

- ▶ The monster has a great sense of direction. It hunts for victims in a large maze.

- ▶ Its red eyes are the last things its victims see.

HARPY

FOUND: GREECE AND ITALY

- ► Harpies are large, woman-faced birds.

- ► Harpies' screeches make their **preys'** mind foggy.

- ► Harpies attack with razor-sharp teeth and claws.

prey—someone or something that is hunted for food

CHIMISIT vs. SPHINX

Would you choose the Chimisit or the Sphinx?

CHIMISIT

FOUND: NANDI, KENYA

- ▶ The Chimisit is a cross between a hyena and a bear.

- ▶ The Chimisit waits in trees on moonless nights to attack.

- ▶ It likes to eat the brains of its victims.

SPHINX

FOUND: EGYPT

- ▶ The Sphinx has a lion's body with a woman's head and chest.

- ▶ Some sphinxes have eagles' wings and snakes' tails.

- ▶ The monster asks a **riddle** to its victims. If the person solves the riddle, he or she can pass without harm. If not, the person becomes the Sphinx's meal.

riddle—a statement or question that makes you think and that often has a surprising answer

ZOMBIE VS. OLGOI-KHORKHOI

Would you rather face a zombie or an olgoi-khorkhoi?

ZOMBIE

FOUND: ANYWHERE THE DEAD SLEEP

▶ Zombies feel no pain. They are focused only on humans, their food.

▶ Just one zombie bite can turn you into a zombie.

▶ Destroying a zombie's brain is the only way to stop it.

OLGOI-KHORKHOI
FOUND: THE GOBI DESERT

▶ An olgoi-khorkhoi is a giant worm 3 to 6 feet (1 to 2 meters) long.

▶ The olgoi-khorkhoi are deadly to touch. They also spit **venom**.

▶ The worms can **electrocute** their victims from far away.

venom—liquid poison made by an animal to kill its prey

electrocute—kill with a severe electric shock

KRAKEN vs. DRAGON

Would you pick a kraken or a dragon?

KRAKEN

FOUND: DEEP SEAS

Some people think the kraken might have been a giant octopus.

► A kraken is larger than the ships it attacks.

► Krakens have two **tentacles** and eight arms. Both are covered in suction cups. The suction cups are lined with rows of sharp teeth.

► When the kraken goes underwater, its body creates a **whirlpool**. The spinning water sucks sailors down.

tentacle—a long, armlike body part some animals use to touch, grab, or smell

whirlpool—a water current that moves rapidly in a circle

DRAGON
FOUND: EUROPE

▶ A dragon's body is covered in hard scales that stop most weapons.

▶ Its claws and teeth can easily cut victims.

▶ Dragons can breathe fire, roasting victims.

WENDIGO VS.
BABA YAGA

Would you rather be controlled by a wendigo or meet Baba Yaga?

WENDIGO

FOUND: NORTH AMERICA

► Wendigos possess humans. The possessed become 10 feet (3 m) tall with yellow, rotting skin.

► Wendigos have an unending hunger for human meat.

► The only way to kill a wendigo is to kill the human too.

BABA YAGA

FOUND: RUSSIA

- ▶ Baba Yaga is an old woman with gray hair. Her nose is so long it reaches the ceiling when she sleeps.

- ▶ Baba Yaga hates bad manners. She punishes anyone who is rude to her.

- ▶ Whoever visits Baba Yaga must complete tasks for her. Those who complete them receive her help. But beware! She will eat anyone who fails.

CHUPACABRA
vs. KELPIE

Would you pick an evil dog or an evil horse?

CHUPACABRA

FOUND: NORTH AND SOUTH AMERICA

▶ The chupacabra looks like a dog. But unlike a dog, it has glowing eyes and razor-sharp fangs.

▶ The monster sucks its prey's blood.

▶ The chupacabra usually attacks farm animals. But if it did attack a human, the result wouldn't be good.

KELPIE

FOUND: SCOTLAND

► Kelpies are evil water **spirits** that can take different shapes.

► They often appear as gentle horses, but they are dangerous. Kelpies trick travelers and drown them in water.

► Kelpies can also appear as humans. In these cases, kelpies will grab victims and drag them under the water.

spirit—a ghost

BASILISK VS. MANTICORE

Would you rather face a basilisk or a manticore?

BASILISK

FOUND: EUROPE

► A basilisk is a snake. It grows about 1 foot (0.3 m) long.

► Its bite and breath are **poisonous**.

► Eye contact with a basilisk is deadly.

poisonous—able to harm or kill if swallowed, inhaled, or touched

MANTICORE

FOUND: MIDDLE EAST

▶ A manticore has a lion's body and a scorpion tail.

▶ Its head is human except for three rows of sharp, pointed teeth.

▶ A manticore's favorite snack is a human. It can swallow one whole.

RAKSHASA vs. FURY

Would you pick a rakshasa or a fury?

▶ Rakshasas are creatures that appear in cemeteries. Rakshasas eat human flesh.

▶ They can take any shape they want, including animals, humans, or monsters.

▶ Their king, Ravana, has 10 heads and 20 arms.

FURY

FOUND: ANYWHERE

- ▶ Furies are the ghosts of murdered women. Furies use their poisonous breath to attack their victims.

- ▶ Bat wings rest on the backs of furies. Instead of hair, snakes hiss from their heads. Their eyes drip blood.

- ▶ They carry whips, cups of venom, and torches.

MANANANGGAL
vs. DULLAHAN

Would you choose a bloodthirsty monster or a headless horseman?

MANANANGGAL

FOUND: PHILIPPINES

▶ These monsters look like humans, except they have large bat wings.

▶ Manananggals like to eat the hearts of unborn babies.

▶ They will also drink the blood of adult humans.

DULLAHAN

FOUND: IRELAND

▶ As the Dullahan rides his horse, he holds his head in one hand. In the other, he holds his whip—a human spine.

▶ Whenever he stops riding, he shouts out a name. Whoever he names dies instantly.

▶ The Dullahan doesn't like to be spied on. If someone does, he throws a bucket of blood on the spy.

OGRE vs. GOLEM

Would you pick an ogre or a golem?

OGRE

FOUND: FRANCE

- ▶ Ogres are famous for their small brains. They're not very smart, but they can easily hurt people.

- ▶ Ogres have large, strong bodies. Ogres' skin is dull gray or green. They are covered in hair.

- ▶ These monsters love snacking on humans, especially children. Ogres hunt at night and hate the sunlight.

GOLEM
FOUND: PRAGUE

► Golems are strong slaves made from clay.

► Escaped golems destroy everything, including people in their path.

► The only way to stop a golem is to say a special **spell**.

spell—a word or words believed to have magical power

RAPID ROUND

Which would you pick for war?
A **DRAGON** OR A **MANTICORE** ?

Which would you pick for a pet?
A **CHUPACABRA** OR A **HARPY** ?

Which would you have dinner with?
A **ZOMBIE** OR A **VAMPIRE** ?

Which would you want to turn into?
A **SPHINX** OR A **FURY** ?

Which would you pick
as your school mascot?
A **BASILISK** OR A **KELPIE** ?

Which would you rather
find in your house?
AN OGRE OR THE **MINOTAUR** ?

Which would you pick as your friend?
THE **DULLAHAN** OR A GOLEM ?

Which would beat the other in a fight?
A MANANANGGAL OR A **RAKSHASA** ?

Which would you want
to meet on vacation?
AN **OLGOI-KHORKHOI** OR A KRAKEN ?

Which would you want as your teacher?
BABA YAGA OR A **WEREWOLF** ?

GLOSSARY

cryptid (KRIP-tihd)—a creature whose existence has not been proven by science

curse (KURS)—an evil spell meant to harm someone

electrocute (i-LEK-truh-kyoot)—to kill with a severe electric shock

fang (FANG)—a long, pointed tooth

myth (MITH)—a story from ancient times

poisonous (POI-zuhn-uhss)—able to harm or kill if swallowed, inhaled, or touched

prey (PRAY)—someone or something that is hunted for food

riddle (RID-uhl)—a statement or question that makes you think and that often has a surprising answer

spell (SPEL)— a word or words believed to have magical power

spirit (SPIHR-it)—a ghost

tentacle (TEN-tuh-kuhl)—a long, armlike body part some animals use to touch, grab, or smell

venom (VEN-uhm)—a liquid poison made by an animal to kill its prey

whirlpool (WURL-pool)—a water current that moves rapidly in a circle

READ MORE

Castellano, Peter. *Vampires.* Monsters! New York: Gareth Stevens Pub., 2016

Doeden, Matt. *The Anatomy of a Dragon.* The World of Dragons. North Mankato, Minn.: Capstone Press, 2013.

Sautter, A. J. *How to Draw Dragons, Trolls, and Other Dangerous Monsters.* Drawing Fantasy Creatures. North Mankato, Minn.: Capstone Press, 2016.

INTERNET SITES

FactHound offers a safe, fun way to find Internet sites related to this book. All of the sites on FactHound have been researched by our staff.

Here's all you do:

Visit *www.facthound.com*

Type in this code: 9781515744726

Super-cool stuff! Check out projects, games and lots more at **www.capstonekids.com**